Published by
*Federation of Family History Societies (Publications) Ltd.*
The Benson Room,
Birmingham and Midland Institute,
Margaret Street,
Birmingham B3 3BS
United Kingdom



ISBN 1-86006-043-9

First published 1997

Printed and bound by
Oxuniprint,
Great Clarendon Street,
Oxford OX2 6DP

**Bas**



SERIES EDITOR
***Pauline M. Litton***

**FEDERATION OF FAMILY HISTORY SOCIETIES**

## CONTENTS

## INTRODUCTION

Before coming into Family History you may not have realised that what you will inevitably do is enter the world of archives. Denis Norden once said that most people think that 'Archives are where Noah keeps his bees'. They have heard the word 'archives' but not having used them have only a very hazy idea of what they are all about. Archives are generally totally ignored and regarded as a useless pile of old paper – or parchment. When you need them, however, your attitude changes. They become all important and you are faced with a mountain of strange factors to assimilate. It is in fact a separate world that only becomes relevant when you need to prove something by documentation. Family historians just beginning their research suddenly realise that they will need to look at more than lists and indexes and the printed word. There is no doubt that archives are daunting at first but with time and patience you can master them and even become an expert in a particular field.

## WHAT ARE ARCHIVES?

Archives are original documents that are preserved because they are of 'continuing administrative use' (i.e. they may still be needed for reference by the organisation which created them). They are not preserved because they may be of interest. The fact that they are of interest is a bonus. They all result from legislation, which requires action, which results in paper or parchment records of that action.

It is essential to remember that documents were not created with you in mind. They are the result of someone gathering together all the paperwork that survives for a particular activity and storing them in one place. Sir Hilary Jenkinson, a previous Deputy Keeper of Public Records and the archivists' guru, defined archives by four points. First, archives are not collected artificially but accumulate in offices for the purposes of administration. Second, they have an inter-relationship with other documents. Third, they are an actual part of the administration which produced them, and fourth, they have remained in unbroken custody. Just as any modern file once closed is kept for reference, that reference becomes less and less necessary but the files aren't thrown away. They are kept because on occasion you still need to refer to them. They are the 'memory' of whatever organisation created them. Even Domesday Book compiled in the 11th century has been called out as evidence in a court of law in this century.

Sir James Grigg, appointed to head a committee of enquiry to review the rules for selection of records for permanent preservation, said that 'the making of adequate arrangements for the preservation of its records is an inescapable duty of a civilised state'. No one can predict when documents are created which potential users will read them in the future. For instance census returns were created to record the numbers of houses, both inhabited and vacant, the numbers of people, both male and female, and married or otherwise, the numbers employed in a particular trade or industry, the numbers living away from their birthplace, be it at home or abroad, and much more.

Superintendent Registrars and enumerators had no idea that the records they created would be scanned minutely for the particulars of individuals or the character of a neighbourhood. That was not their brief. Because those records were collected locally by pre-designated administrative areas they are stored in that way, topographically. We as family historians have then to use those records when looking for named individuals by recognising that structure and finding our way around it to suit our own purposes.

Documents come in many shapes and forms from the small tightly rolled strips of parchment which record a man's inventory of goods when his executor seeks a grant of probate, to a modern file of papers secured by a treasury tag and originating from Whitehall. Part of the archive may also be the container in which the documents were kept when in use such as the oak-lined iron-bound chest used to store Domesday Book, or the exhibits brought into court as evidence which may be a piece of paper but which also could be jewellery, a bar of soap or an article of clothing. Whatever their form they are the result of someone keeping the evidence of their work as a record of what has been achieved and policies formed. Not all individuals or organisations bother to keep a record for more than a few years – the waste paper syndrome again.

More and more people, however, are now becoming aware of the fact that unless such papers are kept there is no means of telling how things were done, when they were done and who did them. There are occasions when it is necessary to record how something was achieved or discarded in the past and without that pile of paper this is not possible. Many people don't recognise their value. Typical is the experience of the record department of the Coal Board, on hearing that yet another mine had closed down. Their first thought was to get over there and rescue its papers. On arriving at the site where demolition was already taking place, they asked a workman where the records were. After some confusion over the meaning of the word record and an explanation that the records sought were not black vinyl but paper, light dawned. 'Oh the papers. We used them to help fill up the mine shaft' – rubble.

Archaeology is a familiar word to everyone. It is quite often mentioned in the media and although most people will leave it at that, they know it is digging up evidence of the past. They don't want to spend hours in a sea of mud, picking debris out of the ground, but they may like to read of the published history which results from the analysis of that debris. Whenever local councils approve the development of a site, archaeologists are alerted and they are given a short space of time to go in and investigate the ground for historical evidence before it is concreted over. Archives, however, have no warning system if they are outside the sphere of government and even then – as in the case of the Coal Board – they can be lost. They are, however, just as important as archaeological evidence. It is from that mine of paper that you can uncover the historical evidence. The only evidence available for earlier years, because the written word was rare, is that of stone, which survives. Witness the recent unearthing of a Roman soldier's letters written – carved on tablets of stone – whilst guarding the outpost of his empire on Hadrian's Wall. Though archaeologists do not have the written word to help them reconstruct the past, they can seek artifacts and build up the picture of an age that way. Later periods are better served. The business of government was recorded, and that may just as well be business with an individual as with a national or local body. This is not just the King's business stemming from Winchester or Westminster but also all the paperwork – or parchment – that survives for a particular administrative activity and which is stored in one place. They may simply be a small accumulation of local documents or cover 96 miles – yes miles – of shelving as those archives do that are looked after by the Public Record Office (PRO).

## WHAT DO THEY LOOK LIKE?

Earlier documents are recorded on parchment – a collective term for either parchment made from sheepskin, or vellum made from calfskin. Paper documents do not show up in any considerable quantity until the 16th century when paper was first manufactured in England. They come in all shapes and sizes and can be difficult to pack in a way that will preserve them without damage and keep them safe from deterioration. Arthur Agarde, one of the sixteenth century Keepers of the Records, wrote that 'the major perils facing records are fire, water, rats and mice and misplacement'. Parchment is tough and has survived for hundreds of years quite successfully but if kept in insuitable conditions can suffer damage from hungry rodents, fire and water when flooded or mildew when damp. Dirt can eat into the surface and careless handling can mean the edges of the documents become mangled as far back as the writing between the margins. Paper is more vulnerable to damage. The older paper made from rags is tougher than paper made from wood pulp. If it does need repair it must be repaired with similar materials. Technology used in repair has improved over the years and sometimes is so good that it is difficult to see the join. Paper documents being repaired are dampened and stretched flat and the fibres of the frayed edges are separated and blended with the fibres of the new patch to be applied so that there is a smooth surface when the job is finished. Paper stacked in boxes must be kept in acid free materials and the papers need to support one another (a box should be filled to ½" above its rim) when the box is shelved on its end. Parchment too has to be repaired with like material and collagen – which to you or me is sausage skin – is the material used. The rule of repair is that nothing shall be added to the writing and nothing subtracted from it. The documents are not restored, just repaired, so that they will survive.

Most records are working documents and therefore completely unadorned. When the PRO staged the exhibition to celebrate the 900th anniversary of Domesday Book, many of the public who visited it walked right by Domesday not realising that the unassuming document in the glass case was the book itself. They expected something showy and colourful complete with masses of gold leaf simply because of the reputation of the document, forgetting that it was a simple working tool of the Court of Receipt in the Exchequer and was the definitive point of reference in any dispute over rights of land tenure.

Before the fifteenth century most of the documents were written in Latin but many appear in Anglo-Norman French. Legal records were still written in Latin up to 1733, except during the Commonwealth and Protectorate, and even then some courts persisted in using the language.

Files that contain folded maps or plans or photographs should have those extracted and stored separately with a dummy put in place to show that something has been taken out and to explain where it can now be found. Folded papers will eventually crack along the fold and information on them will be lost forever. Extracted maps or plans are stored flat or rolled so that this sort of damage cannot occur again. Photographs need to be stored in envelopes that will not cause an alteration to the image as the document ages. Early photographs were often put into glassine paper envelopes (it looks something like grease-proof paper) and this eventually caused a mark on the photograph along the seam line of the envelope.

You should never attempt to repair documents with sticky tape, even of the archival variety. It will eventually discolour and dry out and you will lose some of the writing or at least obscure it. Similarly if you leave papers gathered by a paper clip or other metal fastener, unless of the non-ferrous variety – which is brass rather than chrome coloured – you will find it rusts and the documents are damaged. Older documents are quite often secured by straight pins which will also rust.

Today we are accustomed to papers punched and tagged into a file cover. Earlier documents were sometimes bound into volumes or at least gathered and stitched together along the binding edge. Mediaeval files were piles of parchments tagged together by a parchment strip or sewn across the top and then rolled up and secured with a tie. Some rolls were formed by stitching the many pieces (called membranes) of parchment together top and bottom and then rolling them up. One of the largest of these weighs about 56 pounds and consists of 500 membranes but the smallest can be a mere four inches wide. The rolls of parchment gave their name to the Rolls room (a former search room in the Public Record Office, Chancery Lane, now closed), the Rolls Estate on which the former Public Record Office was built, the Master of the Rolls (the senior Chancery judge and keeper of the rolls), the Liberty of the Rolls etc. etc. When you hear the name rolls mentioned in connection with archives think of neat rolls of parchment membranes and not Swiss, sausage, bread, cheese etc.

## HOW A DOCUMENT IS SELECTED

Not all records are selected for permanent preservation, only those ones that may be referred to again in a court of law or by an originating body. National documents are 'weeded' as part of an ongoing selection process until they are ready – those that survive the weeding – to be made available to those who wish to consult them. Once a government file is closed, which nowadays is five years after it is opened (even if the matter with which it is concerned is ongoing), a new one is opened for the following five years. When the files are closed some may already have been ear-marked for destruction and some for permanent preservation. What normally happens is that the file is stored for five more years and then it is reviewed. If after this period it is deemed to be no longer necessary for the transaction of the business with which it is concerned, then it is destroyed. Those files that survive this 'First Review' are stored for a further twenty years when they are reviewed again and more files are weeded out and destroyed. It is only those that survive the second review which are kept for ever. Normally they are first made available to the public five years later, when they are thirty years older than the last piece of paper attached to the file. This is known as the 'Thirty Year Rule'. During this time they are cleaned, numbered, packed and listed ready for production to the public. This means that they only become available on the first working day of the year immediately after the thirty years have elapsed. The 1891 census, for example, did not become available until 2nd January 1992.

## EXTENDED CLOSURE

Some files in the selection, however, will be deemed to contain sensitive information and they are closed for a longer period (known as Extended Closure). This may be 50, 75 or 100 years from the date of the closure of the file as decreed by the Advisory Council on Public Records. The sensitivity perceived may be to do with national security or to do with personal privacy. Census returns are collected on the understanding that any information given to the enumerator is confidential and it cannot, therefore, be breached within the anticipated lifetime of the person being enumerated. Hence the 100 year closure they are subjected to. We may think this is excessive given the nature of most of the information filled in on the schedule but having given a confidentiality assurance the government cannot go back on its word without an additional Act of Parliament. It is no good saying that in the light of current thinking this degree of confidentiality is excessive; the confidentiality clause was written into the original act for the taking of any particular census.

## PREPARATION AND PACKING

Once documents have been selected for retention they need to be prepared so they can sit on their shelf without further deterioration for ever. Anyone who has seen a pile of unsorted and unidentified documents awaiting accessioning cannot imagine how they are brought into some kind of order so that an individual item can be selected and consulted. Files and bundles of records may have been kept in good conditions and be relatively clean and well cared for. There are those, however, that have suffered from neglect, that are dirty and crumpled with no means of identification, and which arrive at a record office in any kind of container with odd pages coming adrift, shedding fragments and generally looking like the waifs and strays they are. When the records of the Prerogative Court of Canterbury were taken into the PRO they weighed 12 tons and masks were required to protect the sorters from inhaling the dust for which vacuum cleaners were provided. The first vacuum cleaners used in the PRO were for documents and not for cleaning the rooms.

First one needs to sort, not rearrange, the pile of records into some kind of order. By this I don't mean destroy the bundles and groupings in which they are found but to discover exactly what documents are there, what dates they cover and whether they are the same kind or would be better separated into two or more classes of records. When the PRO was set up in the 1850s many of the documents taken in were in this raw state and they had to be sorted, stamped, numbered, labelled, flattened, cleaned, boxed and listed. Nowadays a lot of this work is done by the parent government departments – but not always. Sometimes records are 'orphaned' due to a change in parent body and the archivists themselves need to prepare the documents for accessioning.

## MEANS OF IDENTIFICATION

The end result of this initial sort is the beginnings of a classification system that will give an individual document a reference. A reference is the name by which it is known and an address on the shelves where it is kept so it can be retrieved. As a former Assistant Keeper at the PRO once said 'it doesn't matter what you call a document as long as it comes when it's called'.

The means of identifying a document vary slightly depending on where they are held. The same principles apply, however, in providing a unique reference for each individual piece of an archive. Documents are generally gathered into groups which relate to where they came from or how they were gathered. This may be the name of the government department that created them, or the law court that produced them, or they may be a collection of private papers collected together by an individual in the course of their career. Each group is given a name which is probably expressed in letters e.g. RG for Registrar General which you will meet when using census returns and Nonconformist registers, because they came from his department.

The group is next divided into classes according to the type of document they are within that group. Papers created by a court of law take many forms such as proceedings, depositions, writs, etc., each one of which will form a separate class of records within a group. There may be several classes of depositions alone, divided by date or the part of the country from whence they came.

Then each item in a class is given a number to distinguish it from its fellows. Put these three items together and you have a document reference. Before modern referencing systems were introduced they were described in detail each time they were taken off the shelf. For instance at the PRO, a potential reader would ask to look at Exchequer documents of the Lord Treasurer's Remembrancer, Particulars and Warrants for Leases, Buckingham. No. 6814. Nowadays you would simply ask for E 367/6814. Or if you asked now for FO 244/10 you would receive what was once called Foreign Office Embassy Archives, Prussia and Germany 1819.

Within a document you may have page numbers and folio numbers, either applied to each folio before microfilming, binding or calendaring, with a foliating machine, or a contemporary penned number every so many pages. If the document is indexed, these numbers will be referred to as they are when you need to identify a specific place in the document for a photocopy. Do not confuse page numbers with folio numbers. A page is one side of a leaf in a book or in a bundle of papers. A folio is both sides of that leaf.

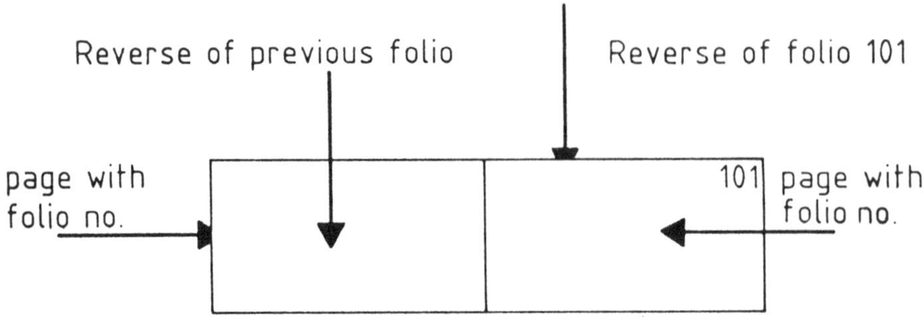


Folio numbers

You will meet folio numbers frequently when searching documents so it is as well to know exactly what is meant by the term.

## FINDING AIDS

This is the term given to those lists and indexes which help you find your way towards the particular document you want to look at. Each class of document will have a listing of its contents but there are different types of list and some lists also have indexes, whether contemporary or modern.

## GUIDES

Before you decide on the class of document you want to read, you will need to consult a guide or listing of the contents of the record office you are in. Nationally, the PRO has a three part guide which lists every class of record it holds, giving a thumbnail sketch of each one, together with an administrative history, to give you an idea of which court or government department is likely to have created the documents you need and an index which cross-refers you to inter-related document classes. This is available in the search rooms as a many volume set of post-binders but it is also available on fiche and may very well be put on the Internet or made available on CD-ROM discs in due course so you can do some homework before you travel to London. Local history libraries and county record offices also publish listings of their holdings. Items come in all the time so it is as well to discover what has been added to the list each time you visit the search rooms.

## CLASS LISTS

A guide will probably identify more than one class of record that may be useful to you. It is, however, only a brief indication of what subject is covered by the records. To discover exactly which record you require you need to go to a class list which will be housed on the shelves of a reading room. These vary tremendously having been written at various times in the style then current.

There are also different types of list: transcripts, calendars, descriptive lists and even packing lists. When record offices were established there was often nothing more than an identification of a class of records – what would become the title of the class. This would be listed simply by a bundle perhaps labelled with the regnal year of when it was written. Many documents are taken in, though not so often nowadays, with no list to accompany them.

## TRANSCRIPT

A transcript of a document is a written copy which follows the abbreviations, punctuation and layout of the original. Nowadays most people want a photocopy of a document but for some types of record this is inappropriate and some other means of reproduction is used instead. You will need to transcribe at least parts of a document, however, if you are indexing.

## CALENDAR

A calendar lists all the documents in a class of records and gives all the essential information such as names and dates but it will not reproduce every word as does a transcript. Used in conjunction with contemporary indexes (q.v.) this may be just as efficient as a transcript to give you the salient points you seek.

## DESCRIPTIVE LIST

Each class of documents is listed to give you not only the full reference for each item, but also a date range and a precis of what the document contains together with a note of its former reference (whilst it was in day to day use) if one survives. The Public Record Office lists are always preceded by an introductory note which will tell you something about how the class of documents came into being and will refer you to other classes of related documents.

## PACKING LIST

A packing list is a very basic list of documents in numerical order of reference and is especially useful to repositories where some of the earlier lists are in some other arrangement than in reference order. These may be topographical groupings such as the list of Nonconformist Registers held by the PRO (RG 4).

## INFORMATION LEAFLET

Archivists generally produce leaflets explaining more popular classes of records or groups of related records. These are for handing out to the public and for enclosures with answers to research queries received by post. It is pointless repeating oneself over and over again when the same questions that require detailed replies occur.

## GUIDEBOOK

Those record offices which produce publications may very well have guidebooks to certain types of records which are heavily used by the public. They will not list the documents concerned but will tell you all you need to know in order to tackle the records with a degree of confidence when you are unfamiliar with them. They tell you how to use the records.

## HANDBOOK

This is a more detailed, in-depth, study of a particular type or grouping of records than is a guide book. It aims to introduce a searcher to the potential of the records and related material rather than talk him through how to use them.

## INDEX

Because of the order in which they are arranged or because of the difficulty in finding a particular item in a bundle of records, some classes have been indexed either nominally, chronologically or topographically, whichever seems the most appropriate. These are compiled to assist searchers who might otherwise spend days looking, as it were, for a needle in a haystack.

## CONTEMPORARY INDEX

Sometimes when documents were still in use, some kind of indexing was required to isolate a particular piece of paper or parchment. In the days before computer indexing this was generally achieved by entering correspondence received, or proceedings filed, into a register. Obviously creating an index in this way, it would be impossible to sort the entries into strict alphabetical order, so they were added to the bottom of a list under the letter of the alphabet. Occasionally this was further divided by the second letter of a word so, for instance, into 'ba', 'be', 'bo' and so on. These 'contemporary indexes' are created whilst the document is still in everyday use so they are contemporaries to the documents to which they refer. They are, therefore, documents themselves and will need to be ordered and consulted before you order the document they refer you to. The entry you find in them will generally give you a name and a number. You have no idea what the number is but need to record it in your notebook so that when you order the document to which it refers, you can locate your particular record by its own peculiar referencing system. The number you picked up from the contemporary indexes will probably be either a folio number, page number, entry number or quire number. Once you look at the structure of the document you will see which numbering system it has and be able to find your particular entry.

## REPRODUCTION

If you are successful with your searches, you may wish to take home a copy of the document you have been working on either to use as evidence of your research, or in order to decipher some handwriting at leisure, to use in an evening class, as teacher or pupil, or to provide an illustration in a publication. If the documents you were looking at are on film then many record offices nowadays have reader/printers that will allow you, for a fee, to make a copy from the microfilm. Simple instructions are generally provided and the fee may be paid across a desk in exchange for a token or by putting a coin in the slot on the machine. If a reader/printer is not available then it may be necessary to go back to the original supplier of the film in order to obtain a copy. Many copies of documents are made available on film, not just to preserve the records from excessive handling where they are held, but also to enable you to view documents of local interest away from the location of the documents themselves. If, however, your document is not filmed you will have to ask the advice of the search room staff. Not all documents can be put onto a photocopier, either because their physical make-up does not allow it – think of putting a roll of parchment on a photocopying machine – or because it is not possible to make a clear reproduction from the document. In either case another means of reproduction, and there are several, will have to be used. The most difficult to read will have to be photographed by a photographer which will mean higher fees. Although some documents could go on to a photocopier, the intensity of light needed to reproduce the writing can seriously damage the original document and fade its ink. Before photocopying was available the only way to make an official copy was to do it by hand and in fact it was one of the first tasks taken on by the clerical staff under training. They had to painstakingly copy everything by hand and were only allowed one mistake per page otherwise the work was scrapped and they had to start again.

## COPYRIGHT

If you purchase a photocopy of a page of a document you will probably find a copyright statement on it or accompanying it. This will point out that the copyright belongs to the Crown or other holding body and that you may not reproduce it without permission of the Copyright holder. If you simply want to have a copy as evidence of your research, there is no problem, you simply file it away. If, however, you wish to use it as an illustration in a publication you need to write and ask for permission to reproduce the photocopy. You will generally be given permission but don't assume it, get the permission in writing. You will probably also be charged a reproduction fee. You will be asked to identify the Copyright holder in the publication and probably be given the correct wording so to do.

You may also wish to use photocopies to provide an exercise in a classroom. Again, in order to provide several copies, one for each pupil, or make an overhead or slide you need to write asking for written permission to do so, clearly stating your purpose. It is quite acceptable to reproduce documents for educational purposes, providing you have written permission, but if there is to be commercial gain made from them, or if you reproduce them without acknowledging the Copyright holder, you could be prosecuted.

## HANDLING

If you are using original archives and not viewing them on film, it is essential that they are handled carefully. There is no back-up copy of anything and although any deterioration can be repaired, the original can never be replaced. For this reason no eating, smoking or drinking is allowed in the searchrooms of any record office. Similarly, you may only write with a pencil and never with a pen. If your pencil needs sharpening, you must do it outside the searchroom. It is as well to correct any mistakes by scoring through your notes rather than erasing the errors as rubber dust does not do documents any good.

The more documents are looked at, the more they are handled and get worn down. Either the natural grease from your fingers or exposure to dust or the crumbling of page edges when they are tamped back into position causes a document to decay. It may seem infinitesimal, even invisible, to you but multiply that by the times a document is produced and the documents can be seriously damaged by the use for which they were kept. You all know how the corner of a book turned down to mark one's place will eventually part company from the page. The same thing happens to the edges of pages of a document if the pages are not all lined up precisely so they will support one another. Eventually the pages will wear back to the writing and when you begin to lose some of the words on the page you are in serious trouble. If you come across a document which has a detached portion of a page lying loose within it, draw it to the attention of the search room officer who can take steps to see it is repaired.

## READERS

Who looks at records besides family historians? The answer is, antiquaries, historians, genealogists, barristers, solicitors, clergymen, record agents, copyists and the general public. Their interests are various: they want copies of court proceedings; evidence of royal grants in Chancery enrolments; private landowners are interested in the history of a manor or in evidence as to rights; family lawyers want evidence of inheritance.

## WHERE ARE DOCUMENTS TO BE FOUND?

Where you are likely to find documents depends on where and why they were written in the first place. Anything produced as part of the day to day work of the government is a national document and will be held at the Public Record Office. Similarly any records of central courts of law will be handed over to the Public Record Office for safe keeping. If a record was created as part of local government or in a county court then it will be found in a local or county records office together with many other documents that could be considered local and not national. Before the public records were moved to the PRO, a potential searcher had to locate where the records were kept just as you do now. In the case of the records of the central courts of law, it was pointed out that to seek a judgement in three courts would have meant the searcher would have to go to six different places to see all the records with no guarantee (remember there were no telephones) of the offices concerned being open when they arrived or that they could find the entrance to each place when they got there. Fees were charged to see the records. The earliest fee book that survives is that of the records kept at the Tower of London. In 1661 a certain Mr. Butler had to pay 10s before he could look for Butler families in Cheshire. It had to be a genealogist, didn't it? Then, as now, documents were essential to the pursuit of genealogy.

## HOW TO ORGANISE YOUR RESEARCH

You will need a notebook in which to record your research. It is a very good idea to record exactly which documents you look at with their exact references, even if your search is unsuccessful, because in the future, when you are planning the next bit of your research, you will not remember what you have already looked at. You should also put your name and address inside the cover of the notebook, just in case you mislay it somewhere. Be methodical, record what you do and what you find, together with the full reference and, most of all, enjoy the searching. You may turn up more than ancestors.

## GLOSSARY

*Finding Aid*

Any list or index which helps you find your way around a class of records and enables you to select an individual item.

*Group Letters*

A term for the alphabetical segment of a document reference. Used in the PRO but also elsewhere. It relates to the government department or court of law from which a document comes.

*Class Number*

A term for the middle segment of a document reference which indicates to which of many classes in a group a document belongs.

*Piece number*

An archival term for an individual unit and its distinguishing number. A unit may be a file, a volume, a map or plan, an exhibit, a roll of parchment or a bundle of papers.

*Reference*

The complete sequence of letters and figures that identifies a particular document and if necessary a particular page in that document e.g. RG 11/3267 or RG11/3267 f. 32, if you have found a specific place in the document that you want to identify. You can be even more specific if you identify the particular page of the folio by following the folio number with 'r' for 'recto' or 'v' for 'verso'. Alternatively if the folio also has page numbers it is perfectly acceptable to use those instead of recto or verso.

*Folio number*

These numbers are stamped on to the top right-hand corner of every other page before the documents are filmed or bound. The page without a stamped number therefore is the reverse of the page with one. It is archivally incorrect to quote the left-hand page of a two page spread by using the folio number on the top right-hand corner of the facing, right-hand, page. A folio number can only be used for the leaf on which it is stamped. (See the diagram on p. 8.) Folio numbers are used to identify specific entries for photocopying, indexing and locating your place on the film. Do not confuse this with the page number.

*Page number*

This is the number applied to each page of a document either by hand or printed on if the document was a form of some kind. It is not to be confused with the folio number which is used after the documents were in daily use and when the documents were being edited or preserved.

*Quire number*

Sometimes found in documents which were originally created from large folded sheets of paper or parchment. They are written on to the top page of a gathering of folded sheets and are not to be confused with the number of pages in a quire of paper which is a quantitative measurement.

*Recto*

The front page of a folio, abbreviated to 'r'.

*Verso* or *dorse*

The back page of a folio, abbreviated to 'v'.

*Membrane*

A sheet or skin of parchment.

*Vellum*

Parchment made from the skin of a calf.

*Parchment*

Either the skin of a sheep used for writing on or the general name for any animal skin treated for that use.

*Rotulet*

A roll of parchment.

*Regnal year*

Each reign was counted from the day when the Sovereign acceeded to the throne so that on the first anniversary of his succession he had completed his first regnal year. Earlier documents are dated by the current regnal year of the Sovereign and not by the calendar date.

*Domesday Book*

This is virtually the earliest public record held by the PRO. It was compiled by order of William I who sent out commissioners to enquire of local courts who owned the manors in their area, how much they were worth and what assets they had. The result was written up county by county, in what came to be known as Domesday Book. It was used as a reference work in the Court of Receipt in the Exchequer and is still cited today when disputes arise over the origins of local rights.

## ARCHIVAL ORGANISATIONS

*Public Record Office.* The repository which holds the records of central government and the central courts of law. Originally based at Chancery Lane, London, it is now housed at Kew. (Public Record Office, Ruskin Avenue, Kew, Richmond, Surrey TW9 4DU.) It holds many records of use to family historians and is essential when doing mediaeval genealogy. It also administers the central London microfilm searchroom where the PROs holdings of Nonconformist registers, estate duty registers, wills of the Prerogative Court of Canterbury and the whole of the census returns for England and Wales, may be seen on microfilm. This is housed at Myddelton House, Myddelton Street, Islington, London EC1R 1UW.

*County and Local Record Offices.* These record repositories hold locally created records of many kinds. If parish records are not still held by the incumbent then they will be found in the local, county or diocesan record office. They will also have maps and directories pertinent to their area and will be the repository where records of County Councils, Quarter Sessions, wills, manor court rolls, marriage licences, local businesses, will have been deposited where they survive.

*British Record Society.* This organisation has existed since 1888. It publishes indexes of groups of historical records, especially probate records. (The British Record Society, Stone Barn Farm, Sutherland Road, Longsdon, Stoke-on-Trent, Staffs ST9 9QD.)

*British Records Association.* Founded in 1932, the BRA advises on and assists in the preservation of records. (The British Records Association, 18 Padbury Court, London E2 7EH.)

*Royal Commission on Historical Manuscripts.* Since 1869 this organisation has reported on records in private ownership. It also directs the National Register of Archives. (Royal Commission on Historical Manuscripts, Quality Court, Chancery Lane, London WC2A 1HP.)

# BIBLIOGRAPHY


*Enjoying Archives.* David Iredale. 1980. Phillimore, Chichester.

*The Parish Chest.* W.E. Tate. 1983. Phillimore, Chichester.

*The Public Record Office 1858–1958.* John D. Cantwell. 1990. HMSO.

*Latin for Local History.* Eileen A. Gooder. Longmans. 8th Impression 1988.

*Handbook of Dates for Students of English History.* C.R. Cheney. 1961.

*A Manual of Archive Administration.* C. Hilary Jenkinson. 1965.

*Examples of English Handwriting 1150–1750.* H.E.P. Grieve. 1959.

*The Record Interpreter.* C.T. Martin. 1892. 1982 facsimile of 2nd edition, 1910. Phillimore.

*Revised Medieval Latin Word List.* R.E. Latham. 1965.

*The Nation's Memory.* Jane Cox. 1988. HMSO.

*Essays in Memory of Sir Hilary Jenkinson.* A.E.J. Hollaender (ed) 1962.

*Indexing for Editors* and *Editing Records for Publication.* R.F. Hunnisett. 1977. British Records Association.

*The Dictionary of Genealogy.* Terrick FitzHugh. 4th Edition. 1995. A&C Black.

*Dictionary of Genealogical Sources in the Public Record Office.* Stella Colwell. 1992. Weidenfeld and Nicolson.

*Genealogical Resources in English Repositories.* Joy Wade Moulton. 1988. Hampton House (USA). With Supplements.

*Guide to the Public Records. Part I. Introductory.* Hilary Jenkinson. 1949. HMSO.

*English Court Hand.* Johnson and Jenkinson.

*Atlas and Index of Parish Registers.* Cecil Humphery-Smith. 2nd Edition. 1995. Phillimore.

*Indexing for Editors.* Roy Hunnisett. 1972. British Records Association No.2.

*The English Archivist.* Jenkinson.

*A Topographical Dictionary of England.* Samuel Lewis. 1831. S. Lewis and Co. or reprinted 1996 by Genealogical Publishing Co. Inc. Baltimore MD USA.

*An Introduction to the Use of the Public Records.* V.H. Galbraith. 1934. OUP.

*How to Read Old Documents.* E.E. Thoyts. Reprint 1972.